Limericks of Edward Lear

Edited by
D. Brewer

'Limericks of Edward Lear'

ISBN-13: 9781447664925
First Edition

Edward Lear
(1812-1888)

There was a Young Lady of Bute

The was a Young Lady of Bute,
Who played on a silver-gilt flute;
She played several jigs,
To her uncle's white pigs,
That amusing Young Lady of Bute.

There was a Young Lady in White

There was a Young Lady in White,
Who looked out at the depths of
the Night;
But the birds of the air
Filled her heart with despair,
And oppressed that Young Lady in
White.

There was a Young Lady of Dorking

There was a Young Lady of Dorking,
Who bought a large bonnet for
walking;
But its colour and size,
So bedazzled her eyes,
That she very soon went back to
Dorking.

There was a Young Lady of Hull

There was a Young Lady of Hull,
Who was chased by a virulent bull;
But she seized on a spade,
And called out, 'Who's afraid?'
Which distracted that virulent bull.

There was a Young Lady of Norway

There was a Young Lady of Norway,
Who casually sat on a doorway;
When the door squeezed her flat,
She exclaimed, 'What of that?'
This courageous Young Lady of
Norway.

There was a Young Lady of Poole

There was a Young Lady of Poole,
Whose soup was excessively cool;
So she put it to boil
By the aid of some oil,
That ingenious Young Lady of
Poole.

There was a Young Lady of Portugal

There was a Young Lady of
Portugal,
Whose ideas were excessively
nautical:
She climbed up a tree,
To examine the sea,
But declared she would never leave
Portugal.

There was a Young Lady of Ryde

There was a Young Lady of Ryde,
Whose shoe-strings were seldom
untied.
She purchased some clogs,
And some small spotted dogs,
And frequently walked about Ryde

There was a Young Lady of Turkey

There was a Young Lady of Turkey,
Who wept when the weather was
murky;
When the day turned out fine,
She ceased to repine,
That capricious Young Lady of
Turkey.

There was a Young Lady of Tyre

There was a Young Lady of Tyre,
Who swept the loud chords of a
lyre;
At the sound of each sweep
She enraptured the deep,
And enchanted the city of Tyre.

There was a Young Lady whose
Bonnet

There was a Young Lady whose
bonnet,
Came untied when the birds sate
upon it;
But she said: 'I don't care!
All the birds in the air
Are welcome to sit on my bonnet!'

There was a Young Lady whose
Chin

There was a Young Lady whose
chin,
Resembled the point of a pin;
So she had it made sharp,
And purchased a harp,
And played several tunes with her
chin.

There was a Young Lady whose
Eyes

There was a Young Lady whose
eyes,
were unique as to colour and size;
When she opened them wide,
people all turned aside,
and started away in surprise.

There was a Young Lady whose
Nose

There was a Young Lady whose
nose,
Was so long that it reached to her
toes;
So she hired an Old Lady,
Whose conduct was steady,
To carry that wonderful nose.

There was a Young Person of Crete

There was a Young Person of Crete,
Whose toilette was far from
complete;
She dressed in a sack,
Spickle-speckled with black,
That ombliferous person of Crete.

There was a Young Person of
Smyrna

There was a Young Person of
Smyrna,
Whose Grandmother threatened to
burn her;
But she seized on the cat,
And said, 'Granny, burn that!
You incongruous Old Woman of
Smyrna!'

There was a Young Person whose
History

There was a Young Person whose
history
Was always considered a mystery.
She sat in a ditch,
Although no one knew which,
And composed a small treatise on
history.

There was an Old Man of Quebec

There was an Old Man of Quebec,
A beetle ran over his neck;
But he cried, 'With a needle,
I'll slay you, O beadle!'
That angry Old Man of Quebec.

There was an Old Derry Down
Derry

There was an Old Derry down
Derry,
Who loved to see little folks merry;
So he made them a Book,
And with laughter they shook,
At the fun of that Derry down
Derry!

There was an Old Lady of Chertsey

There was an Old Lady of Chertsey,
Who made a remarkable curtsey;
She twirled round and round,
Till she sunk underground,
Which distressed all the people of
Chertsey.

There was an Old Lady of
Winchelsea

There was an Old Lady of
Winchelsea,
Who said, 'If you needle or pin shall
see
On the floor of my room,
Sweep it up with the broom!'
That exhaustive old Lady of
Winchelsea!

There was an Old Lady whose Folly

There was an Old Lady whose folly
Induced her to sit in a holly:
Whereupon by a thorn
Her dress being torn,
She quickly became melancholy.

There was an Old Man in a Boat

There was an Old Man in a boat,
Who said, 'I'm afloat! I'm afloat!'
When they said, 'No! you aint!'
He was ready to faint,
That unhappy Old Man in a boat.

There was an Old Man in a Tree

There was an Old Man in a tree,
Who was horribly bored by a bee.
When they said "Does it buzz?"
He replied "Yes, it does!
It's a regular brute of a bee!"

There was an Old Man of Apulia

There was an Old Man of Apulia,
Whose conduct was very peculiar
He fed twenty sons,
Upon nothing but buns,
That whimsical Man of Apulia.

There was an Old Man of Bohemia

There was an Old Man of Bohemia,
Whose daughter was christened
Euphemia,
Till one day, to his grief,
She married a thief,
Which grieved that Old Man of
Bohemia.

There was an Old Man of Calcutta

There was an Old Man of Calcutta,
Who perpetually ate bread and
butter;
Till a great bit of muffin,
On which he was stuffing,
Choked that horrid old man of
Calcutta.

There was an Old Man of Cape Horn

There was an Old Man of Cape
Horn,
Who wished he had never been
born;
So he sat on a chair,
Till he died of despair,
That dolorous Man of Cape Horn.

There was an Old Man of Coblenz

There was an Old Man of Coblenz,
The length of whose legs was
immense;
He went with one prance
From Turkey to France,
That surprising Old Man of
Coblenz.

There was an Old Man of Columbia

There was an Old Man of
Columbia,
Who was thirsty, and called out for
some beer;
But they brought it quite hot,
In a small copper pot,
Which disgusted that man of
Columbia.

There was an Old Man of Corfu

There was an Old Man of Corfu,
Who never knew what he should
do;
So he rushed up and down,
Till the sun made him brown,
That bewildered Old Man of Corfu.

There was an Old Man of Dundee

There was an Old Man of Dundee,
Who frequented the top of a tree;
When disturbed by the crows,
He abruptly arose,
And exclaimed, 'I'll return to
Dundee.'

There was an Old Man of Hong
Kong

There was an Old Man of Hong
Kong,
Who never did anything wrong.
He lay on his back,
With his head in a sack,
That innocuous Old Man of Hong
Kong.

There was an Old Man of Jamaica

There was an Old Man of Jamaica,
Who suddenly married a Quaker;
But she cried out, 'Alack!
I have married a black!'
Which distressed that Old Man of
Jamaica

There was an Old Man of
Kamschatka

There was an Old Man of
Kamschatka,
Who possessed a remarkable fat
cur;
His gait and his waddle
Were held as a model
To all the fat dogs in Kamschatka.

There was an Old Man of Kildare

There was an Old Man of Kildare,
Who climbed into a very old chair;
When he said,-- "Here I stays,--
till the end of my days,"
That immovable Man of Kildare.

There was an Old Man of Kilkenny

There was an Old Man of Kilkenny,
Who never had more than a penny;
He spent all that money,
In onions and honey,
That wayward Old Man of Kilkenny.

There was an Old Man of Leghorn

There was an Old Man of Leghorn,
The smallest that ever was born;
But quickly snapped up he
Was once by a puppy,
Who devoured that Old Man of
Leghorn.

There was an Old Man of Madras

There was an Old Man of Madras,
Who rode on a cream-coloured
ass;
But the length of its ears,
So promoted his fears,
That it killed that Old Man of
Madras.

There was an Old Man of Melrose

There was an Old Man of Melrose,
Who walked on the tips of his toes;
But they said, 'It ain't pleasant,
To see you at present,
You stupid Old Man of Melrose.

There was an Old Man of Moldavia

There was an Old Man of Moldavia,
Who had the most curious
behaviour;
For while he was able,
He slept on a table.
That funny Old Man of Moldavia.

There was an Old Man of Nepaul

There was an Old Man of Nepaul,
From his horse had a terrible fall;
But, though split quite in two,
By some very strong glue,
They mended that Man of Nepaul.

There was an Old Man of New York

There was an Old Man of New
York,
Who murdered himself with a fork;
But nobody cried
though he very soon died,-
For that silly Old Man of New York.

There was an Old Man of Peru

There was an Old Man of Peru,
Who never knew what he should
do;
So he tore off his hair,
And behaved like a bear,
That intrinsic Old Man of Peru.

There was an Old Man of th'
Abruzzi

There was an Old Man of th'
Abruzzi,
So blind that he couldn't his foot
see;
When they said, 'That's your toe,'
He replied, 'Is it so?'
That doubtful Old Man of th'
Abruzzi.

There was an Old Man of the Dee

There was an Old Man of the Dee,
Who was sadly annoyed by a flea;
When he said, 'I will scratch it,'
They gave him a hatchet,
Which grieved that Old Man of the
Dee.

There was an Old Man of the East

There was an Old Man of the East,
Who gave all his children a feast;
But they all ate so much
And their conduct was such
That it killed that Old Man of the
East

There was an Old Man of the
Hague

There was an Old Man of the
Hague,
Whose ideas were excessively
vague;
He built a balloon
To examine the moon,
That deluded Old Man of the
Hague.

There was an Old Man of the Isles

There was an Old Man of the Isles,
Whose face was pervaded with
smiles;
He sung high dum diddle,
And played on the fiddle,
That amiable Man of the Isles.

There was an Old Man of the Nile

There was an Old Man of the Nile,
Who sharpened his nails with a file,
Till he cut out his thumbs,
And said calmly, 'This comes
Of sharpening one's nails with a
file!'

There was an Old Man of the North

There was an Old Man of the
North,
Who fell into a basin of broth;
But a laudable cook,
Fished him out with a hook,
Which saved that Old Man of the
North

There was an Old Man of the South

There was an Old Man of the
South,
Who had an immoderate mouth;
But in swallowing a dish,
That was quite full of fish,
He was choked, that Old Man of
the South.

There was an Old Man of the West

There was an Old Man of the West,
Who wore a pale plum-coloured
vest;
When they said, 'Does it fit?'
He replied, 'Not a bit!'
That uneasy Old Man of the West.

There was an Old Man of the Wrekin

There was an Old Man of the
Wrekin
Whose shoes made a horrible
creaking
But they said, 'Tell us whether,
Your shoes are of leather,
Or of what, you Old Man of the
Wrekin?'

There was an Old Man of
Thermopylæ

There was an Old Man of
Thermopylæ,
Who never did anything properly;
But they said, "If you choose,
To boil eggs in your shoes,
You shall never remain in
Thermopylæ."

There was an Old Man of Tobago

There was an Old Man of Tobago,
Who lived on rice, gruel and sago
Till, much to his bliss,
His physician said this -
To a leg, sir, of mutton you may go.

There was an Old Man of Vesuvius

There was an Old Man of Vesuvius,
Who studied the works of
Vitruvius;
When the flames burnt his book,
To drinking he took,
That morbid Old Man of Vesuvius.

There was an Old Man of Vienna

There was an Old Man of Vienna,
Who lived upon Tincture of Senna;
When that did not agree,
He took Camomile Tea,
That nasty Old Man of Vienna.

There was an Old Man on a Hill

There was an Old Man on a hill,
Who seldom, if ever, stood still;
He ran up and down,
In his Grandmother's gown,
Which adorned that Old Man on a
hill.

There was an Old Man on some
Rocks

There was an Old Man on some
rocks,
Who shut his wife up in a box;
When she said, 'Let me out!'
He exclaimed, 'Without doubt,
You will pass all your life in that
box.'

There was an Old Man on the Border

There was an Old Man on the
Border,
Who lived in the utmost disorder;
He danced with the cat,
and made tea in his hat,
Which vexed all the folks on the
Border.

There was an Old Man who Felt Pert

There was an Old Man who felt
pert
When he wore a pale rose-
coloured shirt.
When they said "Is it pleasant?"
He cried "Not at present--
It's a little to short -- is my shirt!"

There was an Old Man who said
'Well!'

There was an Old Man who said,
'Well!
Will nobody answer this bell?
I have pulled day and night,
Till my hair has grown white,
But nobody answers this bell!'

There was an Old Man who said
'How'

There was an Old Man who said,
'How
Shall I flee from that horrible cow?
I will sit on this stile,
And continue to smile,
Which may soften the heart of that
cow.'

There was an Old Man who said
'Hush!'

There was an Old Man who said,
'Hush!
I perceive a young bird in this
bush!'
When they said, 'Is it small?'
He replied, 'Not at all!
It is four times as big as the bush!'

There was an Old Man who
Supposed

There was an Old Man who
supposed,
That the street door was partially
closed;
But some very large rats,
Ate his coats and his hats,
While that futile old gentleman
dozed.

There was an Old Man who, When
Little

There was an Old Man who, when
little,
Fell casually into a Kettle;
But, growing too stout,
He could never get out,
So he passed all his life in that
Kettle.

There was an Old Man Whose
Despair

There was an Old Man whose
despair
Induced him to purchase a hare:
Whereon one fine day,
He rode wholly away,
Which partly assuaged his despair.

There was an Old Man with a Beard

There was an Old Man with a
beard,
Who said, 'It is just as I feared!
Two Owls and a Hen,
Four Larks and a Wren,
Have all built their nests in my
beard!'

There was an Old Man with a Flute

There was an Old Man with a flute,
A serpent ran into his boot;
But he played day and night,
Till the serpent took flight,
And avoided that man with a flute.

There was an Old Man with a Gong

There was an Old Man with a gong,
Who bumped at it all day long;
But they called out, 'O law!
You're a horrid old bore!'
So they smashed that Old Man
with a gong.

There was an Old Man with a Nose

There was an Old Man with a nose,
Who said, 'If you choose to
suppose,
That my nose is too long,
You are certainly wrong!'
That remarkable Man with a nose.

There was an Old Person In Black

There was an Old Person in Black,
A Grasshopper jumped on his back;
When it chirped in his ear,
He was smitten with fear,
That helpless Old Person in Black.

There was an Old Person in Gray

There was an Old Person in Gray,
Whose feelings were tinged with
disman;
She purchased two Parrots,
And fed them with Carrots,
Which pleased that Old Person in
Gray.

There was an Old Person of Bangor

There was an Old Person of
Bangor,
Whose face was distorted with
anger!
He tore off his boots,
And subsisted on roots,
That irascible Person of Bangor.

There was an Old Person of Basing

There was an Old Person of Basing,
Whose presence of mind was
amazing;
He purchased a steed,
Which he rode at full speed,
And escaped from the people of
Basing.

There was an Old Person of Buda

There was an Old Person of Buda,
Whose conduct grew ruder and
ruder;
Till at last, with a hammer,
They silenced his clamour,
By smashing that Person of Buda.

There was an Old Person of Cadiz

There was an Old Person of Cadiz,
Who was always polite to all ladies;
But in handing his daughter,
He fell into the water,
Which drowned that Old Person of
Cadiz.

There was an Old Person of Chili

There was an Old Person of Chili,
Whose conduct was painful and
silly,
He sate on the stairs,
Eating apples and pears,
That imprudent Old Person of Chili.

There was an Old Person of Cromer

There was an Old Person of
Cromer,
Who stood on one leg to read
Homer;
When he found he grew stiff,
He jumped over the cliff,
Which concluded that Person of
Cromer.

There was an Old Person of Dover

There was an Old Person of Dover,
Who rushed through a field of blue
Clover;
But some very large bees,
Stung his nose and his knees,
So he very soon went back to
Dover.

There was an Old Person of Dutton

There was an Old Person of Dutton,
Whose head was as small as a
button,
So, to make it look big,
He purchased a wig,
And rapidly rushed about Dutton.

There was an Old Person of Hurst

There was an Old Person of Hurst,
Who drank when he was not
athirst;
When they said, 'You'll grow
fatter,'
He answered, 'What matter?'
That globular Person of Hurst.

There was an Old Person of Ischia

There was an Old Person of Ischia,
Whose conduct grew friskier and
friskier;
He dance hornpipes and jigs,
And ate thousands of figs,
That lively Old Person of Ischia.

There was an Old Person of Leeds

There was an Old Person of Leeds,
Whose head was infested with
beads;
She sat on a stool,
And ate gooseberry fool,
Which agreed with that person of
Leeds.

There was an Old Person of Mold

There was an Old Person of Mold,
Who shrank from sensations of
cold,
So he purchased some muffs,
Some furs and some fluffs,
And wrapped himself from the
cold.

There was an Old Person of Nice

There was an Old Person of Nice,
Whose associates were usually
Geese.
They walked out together,
in all sorts of weather.
That affable person of Nice!

There was an Old Person of Paxo

There was an Old Person of Paxo
Which complained when the fleas
bit his back so,
But they gave him a chair
And impelled him to swear,
Which relieved that old person of
Paxo.

There was an Old Person of Philæ

There was an Old Person of Philæ,
Whose conduct was scroobious
and wily;
He rushed up a Palm,
When the weather was calm,
And observed all the ruins of Philæ.

There was an Old Person of Prague

There was an Old Person of Prague,
Who was suddenly seized with the
Plague;
But they gave his some butter,
Which caused him to mutter,
And cured that Old Person of
Prague.

There was an Old Person of Rheims

There was an Old Person of
Rheims,
Who was troubled with horrible
dreams;
So, to keep him awake
They fed him on cake,
Which amused that Old Person of
Rheims.

There was an Old Person of Rhodes

There was an Old Person of
Rhodes,
Who strongly objected to toads;
He paid several cousins,
To catch them by the dozens,
That futile Old Person of Rhodes.

There was an Old Person of Tring

There was an Old Person of Tring,
Who embellished his nose with a
ring;
Ha gazed at the moon
Every evening in June,
That ecstatic Old Person of Tring.

There was an Old Person of Troy

There was an Old Person of Troy,
Whose drink was warm brandy and
soy,
Which he took with a spoon,
By the light of the moon,
In sight of the city of Troy.

There was an Old Person of Wick

There was an Old Person of Wick,
Who said, 'Tick-a-Tick, Tick-a-Tick;
Chickabee, Chickabaw.'
And he said nothing more,
That laconic Old Person of Wick

There was an Old Person whose Habits

There was an Old Person whose
habits,
Induced him to feed upon rabbits;
When he'd eaten eighteen,
He turned perfectly green,
Upon which he relinquished those
habits.

There was an Old Sailor of Compton

There was an Old Sailor of
Compton,
Whose vessel a rock it once
bump'd on;
The shock was so great,
that it damaged the pate,
Of that singular Sailor of Compton.

There was an Old Man in a Pew

There was Old Man in a pew,
Whose waistcoat was spotted with
blue;
But he tore it in pieces
To give to his nieces,
That cheerful Old Man in a pew.

There was a Young Girl of Majorca

There was a Young Girl of Majorca,
Whose aunt was a very fast walker;
She walked seventy miles,
And leaped fifteen stiles,
Which astonished that Girl of
Majorca.

There was a Young Lady of Clare

There was a Young Lady of Clare,
Who was sadly pursued by a bear;
When she found she was tired,
She abruptly expired,
That unfortunate Lady of Clare.

There was a Young Lady of Lucca

There was a Young Lady of Lucca,
Whose lovers completely forsook
her;
She ran up a tree,
And said, 'Fiddle-de-dee!'
Which embarrassed the people of
Lucca.

There was a Young Lady of Parma

There was a Young Lady of Parma,
Whose conduct grew calmer and
calmer;
When they said, 'Are you dumb?'
She merely said, 'Hum!'
That provoking Young Lady of
Parma.

There was a Young Lady of Russia

There was a Young Lady of Russia,
Who screamed so that no one
could hush her;
Her screams were extreme,--
No one heard such a scream
As was screamed by that Lady from
Russia.

There was a Young Lady of Sweden

There was a Young Lady of
Sweden,
Who went by the slow rain to
Weedon;
When they cried, 'Weedon
Station!'
She made no observation
But thought she should go back to
Sweden.

There was a Young Lady of Troy

There was a Young Lady of Troy,
Whom several large flies did
annoy;
Some she killed with a thump,
Some she drowned at the pump,
And some she took with her to
Troy.

There was a Young Lady of Wales

There was a Young Lady of Wales,
Who caught a large fish without
scales;
When she lifted her hook
She exclaimed, 'Only look!'
That ecstatic Young Lady of Wales.

There was a Young Lady of Welling

There was a Young Lady of Welling,
Whose praise all the world was a-
telling;
She played on a harp,
And caught several carp,
That accomplished Young Lady of
Welling

There was an Old Lady of Prague

There was an Old Lady of Prague,
Whose language was horribly
vague;
When they said, 'Are these caps?'
She answered, 'Perhaps!'
That oracular Lady of Prague.

There was an Old Man at a
Casement

There was an Old Man at a
casement,
Who held up his hands in
amazement;
When they said, 'Sir, you'll fall!'
He replied, 'Not at all!'
That incipient Old Man at a
casement.

There was an Old Man of Aôsta

There was an Old Man of Aôsta,
Who possessed a large cow, but he
lost her;
But they said, 'Don't you see
She has rushed up a tree?
You invidious Old Man of Aôsta!'

There was an Old Man of
Marseilles

There was an Old Man of
Marseilles,
Whose daughters wore bottle-
green veils;
They caught several Fish,
Which they put in a dish,
And sent to their Pa' at Marseilles.

There was an Old Man of the Cape

There was an Old Man of the Cape,
Who possessed a large Barbary
ape,
Till the ape one dark night
Set the house all alight,
Which burned that Old Man of the
Cape.

There was an Old Man of the Coast

There was an Old Man of the coast,
Who placidly sat on a post;
But when it was cold
He relinquished his hold
And called for some hot buttered
toast.

There was an Old Man of
Whitehaven

There was an Old Man of
Whitehaven,
Who danced a quadrille with a
raven;
But they said, 'It's absurd
To encourage this bird!'
So they smashed that Old Man of
Whitehaven.

There was an Old Man with a Beard

There was an Old Man with a
beard,
Who sat on a horse when he
reared;
But they said, "Never mind!
You will fall off behind,
You propitious Old Man with a
beard!"

There was an Old Man with an Owl

There was an Old Man with an owl,
Who continued to bother and
howl;
He sat on a rail
And imbibed bitter ale,
Which refreshed that Old Man and
his owl.

There was an Old Man on whose
Nose

There was an Old Man, on whose
nose,
Most birds of the air could repose;
But they all flew away
At the closing of day,
Which relieved that Old Man and
his nose.

There was an Old Person of Gretna

There was an Old Person of Gretna,
Who rushed down the crater of
Etna;
When they said, 'Is it hot?'
He replied, 'No, it's not!'
That mendacious Old Person of
Gretna.

There was an Old Person of
Anerley

There was an Old Person of
Anerley,
Whose conduct was strange and
unmannerly;
He rushed down the Strand
With a pig in each hand,
But returned in the evening to
Anerley.

There was an Old Person of Berlin

There was an Old Person of Berlin,
Whose form was uncommonly
thin;
Till he once, by mistake,
Was mixed up in a cake,
So they baked that Old Man of
Berlin.

There was an Old Person of Burton

There was an Old Person of Burton,
Whose answers were rather
uncertain;
When they said, 'How d'ye do?'
He replied, 'Who are you?'
That distressing Old Person of
Burton.

There was an Old Person of
Cheadle

There was an Old Person of
Cheadle,
Who was put in the stocks by the
beadle
For stealing some pigs,
Some coats, and some wigs,
That horrible person of Cheadle.

There was an Old Person of
Chester

There was an Old Person of
Chester,
Whom several small children did
pester;
They threw some large stones,
Which broke most of his bones,
And displeased that Old Person of
Chester.

There was an Old Person of Ems

There was an Old Person of Ems,
Who casually fell in the Thames;
And when he was found
They said he was drowned,
That unlucky Old Person of Ems

There was an Old Person of ewell

There was an Old Person of Ewell,
Who chiefly subsisted on gruel;
But to make it more nice
He inserted some mice,
Which refreshed that Old Person of
Ewell.

There was an Old Person of Spain

There was an Old Person of Spain,
Who hated all trouble and pain;
So he sat on a chair,
With his feet in the air,
That umbrageous Old Person of
Spain.

There was an Old Person of Sparta

There was an Old Person of Sparta,
Who had twenty-one sons and one
'darter';
He fed them on snails,
And weighed them in scales,
That wonderful Person of Sparta.

There was an Old Person of Tartary

There was an Old Person of
Tartary,
Who divided his jugular artery;
But he screeched to his wife,
And she said, 'Oh, my life!
Your death will be felt by all
Tartary!'

Ingram Content Group UK Ltd.
Milton Keynes UK
UKHW022150160623
423577UK00012B/859